Decorated by Design

Returning to the Beauty Within

By

Sahibzada

Copyright © *Sahibzada*, 2025
All Rights Reserved

This book is subject to the condition that no part of this book is to be reproduced, transmitted in any form or means; electronic or mechanical, stored in a retrieval system, photocopied, recorded, scanned, or otherwise. Any of these actions require the proper written permission of the author.

Table of Contents

Introduction 1

Chapter 1: The Instinct to Decorate 2

Chapter 2: When Expression Becomes Etching 4

Chapter 3: Designed Already – The Divine Blueprint 6

Chapter 4: Islam & the Art of Clothing 9

Chapter 5: The Psychology of Return 12

Chapter 6: Bare, but Not Lost 14

Chapter 7: Covered in Light 17

Chapter 8: Decorated by Design — Returning to the Beauty Within 20

To every soul searching for beauty outside -

May you remember:

you were already decorated within.

Introduction

We are all born with a need — not just to exist, but to be seen.

To feel beautiful. To be recognized. To express what words sometimes cannot say.

And somewhere along the path of life, we begin to decorate. With clothes, colours, accessories... and sometimes — with permanent marks on the body.

But this book is not a judgment. It is a reminder.

That even before you touched your skin, God had already decorated you. Not with ink or metal, but with meaning. With symmetry. With soul.

The journey ahead is not about guilt. It's about guidance.

Whether you are marked, unmarked, wondering, or healing — this book welcomes you.

It holds space for your questions and offers a quiet return to your original design — beautiful, intentional, whole.

Read slowly. Reflect deeply. May each chapter bring you closer to your inner beauty and to the
One who designed you by purpose.

—Sahibzada

Chapter 1:
The Instinct to Decorate

Humans are not just made to live – we are made to express. To exist beautifully. To be seen with meaning. And to carry an outer reflection of our inner truth.

This is not ego. This is not vanity. It is fitrah – the natural design of the soul.

From the very beginning, humans adorned themselves. With leaves, fabrics, metals, colors, patterns... Not to hide, but to highlight.

Every culture, every age, every land – they all decorated themselves. Because decoration is not modern – it is eternal. A whisper from within that says: *'Let me be seen in a way that reflects who I am.'*

That's why a child smiles when you dress them in something beautiful. That's why adults stand taller in clothes that feel like them. That's why we choose colours that match our moods. Because the body is a canvas – and the soul wants to paint.

But not all decoration is light. Some come from pain. From brokenness. From a craving not to express the soul... but to fill the silence.

And this is where the instinct to decorate begins to shift – from celebration... to compensation.

When beauty becomes burden, and silence feels like emptiness, the human soul searches for something more permanent – something to hold the weight of feeling seen.

And in that moment, the skin becomes a journal. A place to write pain, memory, meaning, rebellion, or love. This is where tattooing begins – not always as rebellion. . . but often as a misguided form of remembrance.

But the truth remains:

You were already decorated... by the One who made you with no flaws in your form and no need for edits.

Chapter 2: When Expression Becomes Etching

There's a moment in every soul's journey when the desire to decorate turns into the desire to define.

When clothing no longer feels enough. When fabric becomes too temporary. When you want something etched – not worn.

That's when the skin becomes a journal. Not to show beauty… but to show a story the world didn't take the time to listen to.

A scar disguised as art. A cry disguised as ink. A silent rebellion, or sometimes… a silent plea. Many think tattooing is just defiance. But often, it's remembrance.
A name, a date, a symbol – things the soul doesn't want to forget. So it burns them into the flesh as if to say:
"Even if the world forgets, I won't."

But remembrance doesn't need to be written on the skin – because the heart is the true vessel of memory. And the mind – when at peace – remembers without scars.

For some, tattooing is about control. When life feels chaotic, we choose where the needle lands. We decide what goes on in our body. We become, for a brief moment, the author of our own image.

But this control is temporary. Because no ink can rewrite the soul. And no design can remove the ache of feeling unseen... unheard... or forgotten.

The soul already came with a mark. A purpose. A design.

Every fingerprint is unique—not because of randomness, but because of intent.

God, the Creator of beauty, has written His signs into our very bodies – from the curve of the eye to the strength in our hands.

You are already tattooed by divine design. You just haven't looked deep enough to see it.

Chapter 3:
Designed Already – The Divine Blueprint

Before you ever wore a shirt, before your skin ever touched fabric, you were already designed. Not by trend. Not by culture. But by the Divine Hand that makes no mistake.

Look at your fingerprint – no two on earth match it. Look at the curve of your ears, the symmetry in your eyes, the architecture of your bones... you are not random. You are written.

In the womb, before you took shape, God already knew your name. Before your body was seen by the world, it was known – fully and intimately – by the One who formed it.

So when you think of marking your body, pause and remember:

You are not a blank canvas. You are a scroll... Already filled with divine detail.

To alter that design – to rewrite what was perfected – is not freedom. It is forgetfulness.

In the Qur'an, God says: *"And in yourselves – do you not see?"* (Surah Adh-Dhariyat 51:21)

Your body is an ayah. A verse. A sign of divine perfection. It breathes, heals, breaks, rebuilds – all without your command.

So when we add tattoos, what are we saying?

Are we improving His design? Are we adding beauty to what He already called "Ahsan Taqweem"

the most perfect form?

No. We are answering pain with a pen that was never meant for skin.

Fitrah is your original state. It is your blueprint. And God does not build anything in need of fixing.

He allows you to decorate – yes. But not by changing the body. He guides you to decorate through what you wear… because that allows the body to remain sacred. God doesn't reject beauty. He protects it. By teaching us:

"You are already enough."

"You don't need to be rewritten — you just need to be remembered."

Chapter 4:
Islam & the Art of Clothing

Islam never denied your urge to decorate – it simply redirected it.

The desire to express beauty, to design, to be seen with grace – that's not forbidden. It's understood. God, the Designer of all things, knew His creation would long for beauty. So He didn't suppress it...

He guided it.

That's why Islam emphasizes clothing – not just as protection but as expression through intention. What you wear is not about hiding. It's about honouring.

Islamic clothing doesn't strip you of identity. It shapes it. It invites you to design yourself with dignity, presence, and poise.

Silk, linen, wool, embroidery, jewels – Islam doesn't deny aesthetics. It elevates them. It invites you to wrap your body in meaning so your body itself remains untouched, sacred, and whole.

In Islam:

Clothes are not a cover of shame. They are a sign of worth.

When you decorate your clothes, you fulfil the same natural urge that tattooing tries to answer — but without the permanence, without the pain, and without rewriting what God has already perfected.

That's why God tells us in the Qur'an: *"O children of Adam, We have bestowed upon you clothing to conceal your private parts and as adornment. . . "* (Surah Al-A'raf 7:26)

Adornment. That means the need is not ignored — it is embraced.

You were meant to be beautiful. But the beauty Islam offers is not based on skin... It's based on presence.
In Islam, your identity isn't in ink — it's in how you walk, how you speak, and how you wrap your soul in outer expression.

That's why the cloak, the jilbab, the turban, the thobe — just these alone are not Islamic clothing.

They are expressions of modesty from certain cultures, yes — but Islam doesn't confine beauty to one style or tradition.

God gave us principles, not restrictions.

For men and women, those principles include modesty, dignity, covering of awrah, and avoidance of arrogance or imitation of the opposite gender.

Any clothing – in any culture – that fulfils those principles becomes Islamic in spirit.

So your beauty doesn't need to look like someone else's. Your dignity doesn't need to match a trend. And your Islamic identity can shine through any fabric that reflects those divine boundaries.

Chapter 5:
The Psychology of Return

No one wakes up one day and decides to tattoo their body.

It begins long before — in the mind, in the heart, in the quiet corners of the self that feel unseen or incomplete.

We reach for ink when words no longer feel enough. We mark the skin when emotions go unwitnessed. We decorate the body because we've forgotten how to decorate the soul.

But returning is not about shame. It's about remembrance.

Tattooing often masks itself as empowerment: *"I'm claiming my body."* But in truth, we tattoo when we feel disconnected from it.

We try to build identity through symbols, shapes, pain, or permanence because we've lost the deeper sense of belonging. Not belonging to society... but to ourselves. To God. To our original form.

That form still exists — untouched beneath the ink.

You don't need to erase the tattoo. You need to heal the belief.

The return doesn't start at the laser clinic. It starts in the mindset. You don't need to punish your past. You need to understand it.

Ask:

- *Why did I mark myself?*

- *What was I trying to say?*

- *What am I ready to release now?*

Because when the need disappears, the ink loses its power.

True return is not physical first — it is psychological. A shift in how you see yourself... and a return to how God sees you.

Chapter 6:
Bare, but Not Lost

Honouring the Soul Beneath the Ink

You may carry tattoos.

You may have chosen markings in the past.

When the pain felt louder than, peace, and ink felt safer than silence.

But let this be said, with love and clarity:

You are not lost,

You are not damaged,

You are not beyond return.

You are simply someone who tried to speak, when no one else was listening.

And now,

You've remembered your voice.

The Tattoo is Not Who You Are

It may live on your skin.

But it does not define your worth. Not to your Creator. Not to your future.

Not to your ability to return with full dignity and grace.

In fact, the act of turning back,

With ink on your body and sincerity in your heart,

Is honoured.

Because it is harder, Because it is real.
And because God sees what's beneath the skin,
Before anyone else sees what's on it.

No Shame in the Journey

You didn't mark your body in sin,

You marked it in search.

And now that you've found the truth... You don't need to erase the past.
You need to reclaim it.

Let your tattoos become reminders,

Not of rebellion,
But of redemption.

Let them say,

"This was once my pain,

But now, it's just part of my story,

Not my identity."

Covered in Grace

You may not be able to remove the mark,
but you can remove the meaning.
You can reclaim your self-worth.

You can return to honouring your body, your presence, your soul.

You can still walk into any gathering,
Into any prayer,
Into any life,

Fully welcomed by God.

Because He is not watching the ink.
He is watching the intention.

And when your heart returns, so does your light.

Chapter 7: Covered in Light

The Radiance of Dignity and Inner Beauty

In a world obsessed with exposure,
choosing to cover is an act of power.
A quiet revolution,
A bold return to dignity over display.

Because when you dress with intention,

Not to attract
Attention, but to
Protect value.
You are not hiding.

You are shining.

Light Is Not What You Show — It's What You Carry

Modesty is not restriction.
It is recognition.
That you are already valuable,
Already beautiful,

Already whole.

You don't have to reveal
everything,
To be respected.
You don't have to bare your body
to express your soul.

God says:
"And tell the believing men and women to lower their gaze and guard their modesty..." "Because purity begins in the eyes before it ever touches the fabric.

True Beauty Has Weight

Real beauty isn't loud.
It's not desperate.
It doesn't demand attention,
it commands it.

The person who walks in covered grace,
Enters the room like a lantern,
Not burning bright,
But glowing steady.
With humility. With presence. With peace.

That's what modesty gives you:
Weight without noise.
Elegance without exposure.
Presence without performance.

The Body is a Temple — and Light Deserves Shelter

When you know your worth,
You don't display it freely.
You don't decorate yourself for consumption,
You design yourself for purpose.

Every fold of fabric becomes a prayer,
Every choice to cover becomes a candle lit in a world,
Starving for truth.
You are not hiding your beauty,
You are placing it where it belongs.

Within the protection of light,
Within the purpose of your creation.

Because what is sacred,
Is always guarded... not exposed.

Chapter 8: Decorated by Design — Returning to the Beauty Within

Returning to the Beauty Within

You were never empty,
Never plain.
Never incomplete.

From the first breath,
You were already enough.
Written, shaped, and presented,
By the greatest artist of all time.

God made no mistake.

Every curve,
Every shade.
Every detail of your form
was intentional.

But in the noise of the world,

In the pressure to be seen,
We forgot.

We tried to add, edit, mark, pierce, and ink,
thinking beauty was something to be achieved,
rather than something to be remembered.

Your Soul Never Needed Saving – Just Remembering
This book was not written to judge those who marked themselves.
It was written to remind the ones who forgot
that they were always marked by purpose.

Not with ink,
But with intention.
Not with scars.
But with soul.

You are already decorated by design.
And when you understand that,
You stop trying to prove your,
beauty and start protecting it.

You dress with dignity.
You walk with grace.
You express,
Not to please the

World…

But to honour your truth.

A Final Whisper

To the one who still wonders …

Who still feels "less than"…

Who still carries the past like a tattoo on the heart.

You are seen.

You are chosen.

You are beautiful.

Just as you were made.

Return not to perfection,

But to your natural state.

The fitrah,

The soul that smiles from within.

The self that doesn't need to scream to be noticed.

This is the true art of being.

You are not missing decoration.

You are the decoration.

A living reminder that design – when divine – needs no addition.

So cover yourself in meaning.
Live with presence.
And shine not by being loud…

… but by being real.

You are — and always have been —
Decorated by Design.

www.ingramcontent.com/pod-product-compliance
Lightning Source LLC
Chambersburg PA
CBHW040731220426
43209CB00086B/1574